# TRUSTING GOD IN MY FAITH WALK

## CAROLYN D. RIGGINS

# Trusting God In My Faith Walk

**ISBN - 978-1-7350504-2-3**

**Copyright - CI-46012450510**

Printed in the United States of America

# Table of Contents

# Dedication

I dedicate this book to all the angels God has blessed me with in my life: my two children, my granddaughter, my daughter-in-law, my sisters, my brother-in-law, my brother, and my mother. To the doctors, nurses, and friends who have supported me. Thank you for being instruments of God's love and grace on my journey.

# Why Read This Book?

This book is a testament to the transformative power of faith and the significance of trusting God through every trial and tribulation. Sharing my personal testimonies and trials has not been easy, but God has laid it on my heart to open up and share my journey. I want others to see that it is through our faith walk that we truly understand the importance of God's presence in our lives.

Throughout my many trials, God's word was my constant source of strength and guidance. Prayer became my lifeline, a direct channel through which I could hear from God. By reading and meditating on His word, I found solace and direction. The scriptures illuminated my path, serving as a beacon of hope and a light of guidance in the darkest times.

In this book, you will see how I navigated through immense challenges by leaning on God's word and trusting in His promises. There were times when the trials seemed unbearable, but through prayer, I found the strength to endure. God's word was not just a source of comfort but a powerful tool that equipped me to face each obstacle with faith and confidence.

You will read about my journey through a painful divorce after 30 years of marriage, my retirement after 27 years of dedicated service, and my venture into starting a business during the uncertainties of the COVID-19 pandemic. You'll also witness my battle with breast cancer for the second time and how I survived a horrendous car accident. Each of these trials tested my faith, but I found the resilience to keep going through prayer, consistent reading, and meditation on God's word.

God's word gave me the wisdom and strength to navigate these challenges. It reminded me that I was not alone and that God had a purpose for each trial. By trusting in His word and relying on prayer, I could see the bigger picture and understand that these tribulations shaped me into a stronger, more faithful individual.

This book is written with sincere compassion and love, aiming to impact and inspire others facing their own trials. Through my story, I hope to convey the profound truth that trusting in God and His word is essential in our faith walk. As you read this book, I pray you will be encouraged to deepen your faith, trust in God's unwavering love, and find strength in His promises.

Faith is not just a belief but an active trust in God's presence and guidance, especially during difficult times. This book highlights the importance of prayer, reading, and meditating on God's word as vital practices that sustain us in our faith journey.

By sharing my experiences, I aim to show how trusting God and His word can lead to incredible transformation and growth.

God has been with me every step of the way, and I am confident He will be with you, too. By sharing my story, I hope to inspire you to trust in God more fully and walk your faith journey confidently, knowing that His word will always be a light to guide you. This book is a testament to the power of faith, the importance of prayer, and the incredible impact of trusting God's word in our faith walk.

# About the Author: Carolyn D. Riggins

Carolyn Riggins's life is a testament to the power of faith, resilience, and compassion. Her unwavering relationship with Jesus Christ as her Lord and Savior is the cornerstone of her existence. She believes wholeheartedly in the gospel's truth and understands the vital importance of sharing its message with others. Her journey has been marked by profound experiences and deep connections, shaping her into the remarkable person she is today.

Carolyn is the proud mother of two children, Joshua and Raven, and the loving mother-in-law to Brittany. Her role as a grandmother to Alana brings her immense joy and fulfillment. She is also a devoted daughter and a cherished sister, always placing family at the heart of her life. Beyond her familial roles, Carolyn is a successful businesswoman, navigating the complexities of the business and management consulting industry with expertise and grace. Her professional achievements are a testament to her dedication and leadership, which have defined her career.

A defining chapter in Carolyn's life is her battle with breast cancer, not once, but twice. Her journey as a two-time breast cancer survivor is a testament to her strength and determination. She faced the trials and tribulations of cancer with unwavering faith, never allowing the disease to deter her from her path. Carolyn's resilience in such adversity has inspired many, demonstrating that one can overcome even the most daunting challenges with faith and perseverance.

Carolyn's life is a tapestry woven with threads of love, compassion, and service. She is a servant of God, committed to living out His word and being a vessel for His purpose. Her compassion for others is evident in every aspect of her life.

She loves people and strives to make a positive difference in their lives. Her caring nature and empathetic heart have touched countless individuals, offering solace and support to those in need.

Transparency is a cornerstone of Carolyn's character. She understands the importance of being open and honest, recognizing that vulnerability is a strength, not a weakness. Her ability to be transparent with others has fostered deep connections and built trust, allowing her to minister effectively and authentically. She is a woman who values the word of God and knows its transformative power. Her faith is a private belief and a guiding force that shapes her actions and interactions with the world.

Throughout her life, Carolyn has embraced the understanding that we all have a purpose. She believes that each of us is called to make a difference in the lives of others and to be a light in the darkness. Her faith walk with God has been her anchor, guiding her through the storms of life and keeping her grounded in hope and love.

Tremendous trials and tribulations have marked Carolyn's journey, but she has never let these challenges stop her. Instead, they have strengthened her resolve and deepened her faith.

Carolyn is a warrior who fights for what is right and just. She stands firm in her beliefs, advocating for truth and justice in all areas of life. Her courage and determination are evident in her actions as she tirelessly works to uplift and empower others. She knows the value of fighting for what is right, even when the odds are against her. Her life is a testament to the power of faith and the importance of standing firm in one's convictions.

As an author, Carolyn uses her experiences and insights to inspire and encourage others. Her writing reflects her journey, filled with wisdom, hope, and the unwavering belief in God's promises. She shares her story with authenticity and grace, offering hope and resilience to those facing their own challenges.

Most of all, Carolyn is a servant of God. Her faith is the foundation of her life, guiding her actions and shaping her character. She understands we are all vessels for God's purpose, calling to serve and love others.

Her life is a testament to this calling, as she continually seeks to impact the world positively. Her journey is one of faith, love, and unwavering commitment to God's word.

Carolyn Riggins stands as a beacon of hope and resilience in a world often uncertain and struggling. Her life story is a powerful reminder that we can overcome obstacles with faith, love, and determination and fulfill our God-given purpose. She is a woman who has walked through the fire and emerged stronger, a true testament to the power of faith and the enduring strength of the human spirit.

# Introduction

In 2020, I found myself at a crossroads, besieged by a series of daunting trials that left me feeling utterly lost. Amidst the tumult, my best friend introduced me to a movie that would become a pivotal turning point in my journey based on *Matthew 6:6 (NIV)*. This film illuminated the extreme importance of having a dedicated space for connecting with God and immersing myself in His word. Inspired by Jesus's words in *Matthew 6:6 (NIV)*, where He instructs us to pray in secret, I created my own war room.

This sacred space became a sanctuary brimming with cherished scriptures, heartfelt prayers, personal reflections, and spiritual books. Here, I prepared for life's battles, seeking intimate moments with God and receiving His guidance, direction, and comfort.

Trusting God in our faith walk is essential. It requires a deep, unwavering commitment to place our lives in His hands, believing He is sovereign over all circumstances. Trusting God means surrendering our struggles to Him, allowing Him to fight our battles, and relying on His wisdom rather than our own. This trust is not passive but active, involving daily decisions to lean on His understanding and seek His will through prayer and scripture.

In my war room, I learned to surrender my struggles to God and let Him fight my battles. This sanctuary quickly became the foundation of my safe haven, where I found peace, happiness, love, and protection through my connection with God. I understood that God is all about love, transformation, and positive change; all He desires is for us to spend time with Him. In this book, I share my journey of relying on God and learning to hear His voice through the daily reading of His word.

God knew His word needed to be deeply rooted in my heart, mind, and soul to prepare me for the battles I would face. He equipped me by guiding me to read, meditate on, and internalize His word. There were times I didn't understand why I was drawn to certain scriptures or felt compelled to pray about specific things, but God knew the path I was about to tread—my faith walks.

My faith walk has not been easy. It has been filled with valleys, dark moments, and painful experiences, but God has supported me through it all. He has lifted me up and strengthened me, reminding me of His loving promises, such as in *Joshua 1:9 (NIV): "Have I not commanded you? Be strong and courageous. Do not be afraid; do not be discouraged, for the Lord your God will be with you wherever you go."*

Spending time with God has been essential for Him to move in my life, help me grow, and mature my faith. I am not a new Christian but a mature believer who continues growing, loving, learning, and sharing His word.

# Trusting God Through Life's Trials

Life is filled with unexpected trials, and trusting God through these times is vital. My journey involved facing significant challenges that tested my faith. A divorce, a second battle with cancer, a car accident, and the uncertainties of starting a new business and retirement were among the obstacles I encountered. Each of these trials, though daunting, served to draw me closer to God, teaching me to depend on Him entirely.

## The Divorce

Divorce is a profoundly painful experience, shaking the very foundations of trust and security. In the aftermath of my divorce, I was left grappling with feelings of failure and rejection. Yet, I found solace in God's promises in these darkest moments. *Psalm 34:18 (NIV) reassured me, "The Lord is close to the brokenhearted and saves those who are crushed in spirit."* Through prayer and scripture, I learned to trust God with my broken heart, allowing His love to heal and restore me.

## Retirement and Starting a New Business

Retirement marks the end of one chapter and the beginning of another. For me, it also meant starting a new business, a venture filled with excitement and uncertainty. This transition required faith, trusting God with my future, and financial security. *Jeremiah 29:11 (NIV) provided assurance: "For I know the plans I have for you," declares the Lord, "plans to prosper you and not to harm you, plans to give you hope and a future."* This promise gave me confidence that God's plans were good and that He would guide me through this new phase of life.

## The Second Cancer Battle

Facing cancer for the second time was a harrowing experience. The fear and uncertainty were overwhelming, but in these moments of vulnerability, I learned to lean on God more than ever. *Isaiah 53:5 (NIV): "But he was pierced for our transgressions, he was crushed for our iniquities; the punishment that brought us peace was on him, and by his wounds we are healed."* This verse became a lifeline, reminding me that God was present in my suffering.

Through prayer, I found the strength to endure treatments and the courage to face each day. Trusting God with my health meant believing in His sovereignty, knowing He held my life in His hands.

### The Car Accident

A car accident can be a jarring and life-altering event. The suddenness and potential for serious injury can evoke fear and anxiety. After my accident, I struggled with these emotions. Still, I also saw it as an opportunity to trust God with my physical well-being and safety. *Proverbs 3:5-6 (NIV) became my anchor: "Trust in the Lord with all your heart and lean not on your own understanding; in all your ways submit to him, and he will make your paths straight."* This scripture taught me to trust God's plan, even when life seemed chaotic and unpredictable.

## A Glimpse into the Journey

As you read through the other chapters of this book, you will journey with me through these trials and witness how trusting God transformed my life. You will see the ups and downs, the moments of doubt, and the triumphs of faith. I hope that by sharing my story, you will be encouraged to trust God in your faith walk, knowing He is with you every step of the way.

In the following pages, you will find a roadmap for your faith journey. You will discover the power of God's word and the importance of prayer. You will see how God uses trials to draw us closer to Him, teaching us to depend on His strength and wisdom. Most importantly, you will be reminded that trusting God is the key to navigating life's challenges with hope and confidence.

# Chapter One: Heartbreaking Divorce and Trusting God Through Heartache

Sitting down to pen my thoughts, I am overwhelmed by mixed emotions. The memories of my past, particularly the heartache, brokenness, and pain that accompanied my divorce, are still vivid in my mind. I was married for 30 years—a lifetime to some. Many might say, "Wow, that's a long time to be married and then get a divorce." Indeed, it was a significant part of my life, and trusting God throughout this journey gave me the support and strength to endure the heartache I experienced.

I want to make it clear from the outset that I do not advocate divorce. Instead, I believe it is crucial for individuals to seek God's guidance and wisdom when making such profound decisions.

It was essential for me to lean completely on God during this difficult period. My faith in God was my rock, anchor, and refuge. It was this unwavering faith that helped me overcome the challenges associated with my divorce. Reflecting on those dark moments before the divorce, I recall feeling emotionally, physically, and spiritually crushed. Divorce, in many ways, felt like death—like losing a part of my heart that no longer functioned. We were no longer one but breaking into many pieces. In those times, I desperately needed God to provide the peace, comfort, and guidance to make it through.

Before the divorce, I prayed fervently for God to give me the strength to navigate the difficult challenges facing our marriage. My marriage was incredibly important, and I was willing to fight for it on my knees. To fight for my marriage, I knew the importance of having a war room. I created a war room to spend time with God, speaking to and hearing from Him. My war room was adorned with my favorite scriptures, which God shared with me to seek guidance in His word. Morning, afternoon, and evening, I pursued God's direction through countless prayers, meditations, and His word studies. I sought God's guidance daily to save our marriage and heal our hearts.

In the war room, I put on my full armor of God. *Ephesians 6:10-17 (NIV)* emphasizes the importance of God's full armor for daily Christian warfare. I felt most safe in my war room with God because it was there that I could pour out my heart, tears, and pain to Him about my life.

I trusted and believed that God would provide me with what I needed. When I was in the war room, I could always depend on God to speak to me when my heart was heavy with pain concerning the difficulties in my marriage. Every day, I was determined to fight for our marriage, knowing that with God's help, anything was possible.

Another scripture I would recite countless times during prayer was *Psalm 32:8 (NIV): "I will instruct you and teach you in the way you should go; I will counsel you with my loving eye on you."* This verse became a daily source of strength and encouragement.

Throughout my journey, I held onto the belief that my love and unwavering commitment to my ex-husband would endure for a lifetime. However, as I navigated this turbulent season, I leaned heavily on seeking God's divine guidance, which became my unwavering anchor. After months of fervent prayer, deep meditation on my circumstances, and immersion in God's teachings, the painful reality of my marriage unfolded into a heartbreaking divorce. The loss of my marriage was indescribable. I felt pain, hurt, disappointment, anger, confusion, emptiness, and failure. I felt like a failure as a wife, a mother, and a Christian.

I was consumed with emotions and felt embarrassed about the loss of my marriage. I struggled to understand what had happened and what my life would look like now. But I also learned that in marriage, both individuals must be willing to fight, pray, and follow God's word together.

I am grateful that God provided the peace and understanding I needed to navigate this difficult path with clarity and acceptance as I continued to trust in His plan for my life.

Going through my divorce taught me many valuable spiritual lessons. Still, the biggest lesson was that forgiveness was necessary for God to bless me and move forward in my faith walk. I had to forgive my ex-husband for the hurt and pain he caused me. God revealed to me that I, too, needed to examine my heart and ask my ex-husband to forgive me for my mistakes and shortcomings.

In *Matthew 6:14-15 (CSB)*, this scripture informs us about forgiveness. God showed me that forgiveness is vital to Him and that we all have a responsibility to forgive one another because He forgives us for our wrongdoings. This was a challenging but essential step for me, as it enabled me to let go of the resentment and pain preventing me from moving forward.

My experience trusting God has shown me that forgiveness is a powerful asset that brings healing, peace, and new beginnings. To move forward and start a new chapter in my life, I needed to let go of the pain, hurt, disappointment, and forgiveness. It was a difficult time in my life, but I had to trust God completely through it all. I am grateful for this experience, as it has helped me to grow closer to God and to understand His love and forgiveness even more.

As I deepened my relationship with God, I began seeing the transformation within me. Even if my marriage ended, I realized that God was still in control of my life and had a greater plan for me. When I understood that God was guiding me along a path specifically designed for me, I began to feel a sense of peace and hope. I found comfort in knowing that God does not abandon us, nor does He ever turn His back on us. He is always there, no matter what.

My divorce was a challenging and painful experience, but it also served as an opportunity for growth and transformation. My faith gave me the strength and courage to face the obstacles head-on. As a result, I am now a more spiritually mature and stronger person. I am thankful for the experiences that allowed my personal development and growth.

I am confident that my relationship with God will continue to guide my path in the years to come. Reflecting on my divorce, I realized that it was not only a personal journey but also a spiritual one. It forced me to dig deep and examine my beliefs, values, and priorities.

I had to confront my fears and uncertainties and trust God's plan. This process was well worth the effort. I was reminded of the importance of living a life centered on my relationship with God. I gained a greater sense of purpose and significance.

One of the most important spiritual lessons I learned was the significance of surrender. I had to release my preconceived notions and relinquish my desire for control, trust God, and allow Him to direct my steps. I realized that I was not alone and that God was walking beside me every step of the way. This humbling experience was also liberating, allowing me to find peace amidst the storm.

I also realized the importance of having a supportive community. Throughout the challenging process of divorce, I was blessed with friends and family who stood by my side. They prayed for me, offered encouragement, shared scriptures, and were there to listen.

I realized that we are not meant to go through life alone, and we all need the support of a loving community to navigate challenging moments.

One of the most meaningful aspects of my faith journey during this time was my quiet moments with God. Whether in the middle of the night or early in the morning, I found comfort as God spoke directly to my heart, offering healing and strength through His precious Word. One scripture that provided me with great comfort was *Psalm 46:10 (NIV): "He says, 'Be still, and know that I am God; I will be exalted among the nations, I will be exalted in the earth."* This verse reminded me of the importance of being still and relying on God, even in difficulty.

Through my divorce, I learned the value of trusting in God and relying on Him during difficult times, even when things seemed bleak. I now share this lesson with others, encouraging them to trust God, pray with their spouse, and read God's Word together. These practices are essential for cultivating a strong relationship with God.

I believe anyone who develops a relationship with God will see a profound transformation in their lives. What I learned most from it was the importance of a relationship with God. Those precious moments with God allowed me to get closer to Him, love Him, and understand Him.

God used the most challenging time of my life to draw me closer to Him. During this time, God poured His word into me, which I desperately needed. I needed God's full armor.

God shifted my focus from my difficulties to Jesus. God showed me how Jesus got through His difficult times through prayer. Jesus never stopped praying. Jesus prayed up to the time of

Judas's betrayal. In *Mark 14:32-39 (CSB)*, Jesus is praying in the garden. If prayer time was important to Jesus, it would also be crucial for us, no matter what life brings. I also learned through my divorce that I needed God's presence to get me through.

I learned the importance of having a relationship with God, trusting Him, and relying on Him for the strength to go through a heartbreaking divorce. There were many times God was present in my life during this time.

Through this experience, my faith was strengthened by the beautiful and fruitful scriptures God provided to help me overcome the challenges and heal my heartache.

If and when you face difficult and challenging moments in your life, I encourage you to trust in God. One powerful scripture that will guide you through is *Proverbs 3:5-6 (NIV): "Trust in the Lord with all your heart and lean not on your own understanding; in all your ways submit to him, and he will make your paths straight."* This verse became my lifeline, and it can be yours too. Trust in God, and He will lead you through the darkest valleys into the light of His love and peace.

# Chapter Two: Retiring from a Long Career – God's Timing is Perfect

For over 35 years, I had the privilege of working in the financial industry—a journey that transformed me in countless ways. Within that timeframe, 27 years at a bank I worked for, God placed me uniquely positioned to share His message of love and hope with those who needed it most.

The opportunity to share my faith with individuals from diverse backgrounds was a privilege that filled my heart with gratitude and awe. I encountered people of different races, genders, ages, and income levels, and each interaction was a chance to share God's word. My heart overflowed with love and compassion for every person I met, and I felt a deep sense of purpose in sharing the gospel.

Not only did I share the gospel with customers, but I also had the opportunity to share it with colleagues, coworkers, and senior management. God gave me the discernment to know when someone needed to hear His word. Through my work, He used me as a platform to reach out to those in need of His message of love and hope.

I was humbled by the thought that God chose me to be a light for Him, to share His love with those I encountered. Seeing how He worked in the lives of others filled me with immense joy and purpose. Positively impacting someone's life through my faith in God was heartwarming, and it was a privilege to be part of His plan to reach those in need.

Reflecting on my career, I am grateful for the amazing ways God used me to share His precious words with others. We often become so focused on our own lives that we forget to thank God for how He uses us to help others. But I have come to understand that it is not about us; it's about serving others and spreading love, just as Jesus did throughout His life.

Jesus demonstrated His love for all of us in countless ways, and I pray that I, too, can share God's word with as many people as possible. Sharing the gospel with others is of utmost importance to me, as I have seen the transformative power of faith in Christ Jesus. By believing in Jesus and accepting Him as their Lord and Savior, individuals can experience a life-changing transformation that only God can bring.

I appreciate the opportunities God has given me to share His message of hope and love, and I am humbled by the thought that He chose me to be a vessel for His work. I know my career was not just a job but a calling, and I will always look back on it with gratitude and love.

As I continue my journey, I trust God's plan for my life. He will continue to guide and use me in ways I cannot imagine. I am grateful for the experiences and memories from my career in the financial industry and the ways God used me to bring healing and hope to others.

I will always be dedicated to spreading His message of love and serving others in any way I can. I was a young and inexperienced teller when I first started in the financial industry. However, God had big plans for me and blessed me with various experiences throughout my career. From customer service representative to loan administrator, assistant manager, manager, hub manager, and regional manager, each role was a blessing from God and a step closer to fulfilling His plan for my life.

As I pursued my career goals, I faced obstacles when applying for management positions. I felt inadequate, lacking the education and experience necessary to qualify for these roles. But I knew that God had created me to be a leader, and I felt a deep calling within me to pursue this path.

I prayed for guidance and direction and took leadership and loan courses to build my resume and prove my leadership abilities.

I also became involved in the community, volunteering and serving in leadership positions to demonstrate my commitment to serving others.

One day, a manager position became available, and I was invited to two interviews. I was told that I met all the qualifications but needed to prove my ability to do business development by bringing in new clients. I felt uncertain, but I knew God had given me the ability to do this job. I prayed for His help and guidance and trusted He would lead me to success.

To my amazement, God blessed me with not just one but three new business accounts and two personal accounts. I felt overwhelmed by His grace and provision. I immediately informed my manager and the market president of my business development. They were impressed by my efforts and offered me my first manager position.

This experience taught me the truth in *Matthew 19:26 (NIV); Jesus looked at them and said, "With man, this is impossible, but with God, all things are possible."* I was filled with gratitude and awe at how God had worked in my life, helping me overcome obstacles and reach my goals. I felt deeply grateful for His guidance and support and was reminded of the incredible power of faith and prayer. I will always look to God for strength and direction, and I am filled with a deep sense of peace and purpose as I continue to follow His plan for my life.

Retiring from a long career was a significant transition, but I trusted God's perfect timing. When God first shared with me that it was time to retire, I was 53 years old and overwhelmed with emotions. I was nervous and scared. I cried for weeks, unable to comprehend the end of this significant chapter of my life. The thought of leaving behind a career that had been so integral to my identity was daunting. I felt an immense weight of uncertainty and fear about what the future held.

As I prepared myself to accept retirement, I grappled with many emotions. I still had over 300 hours of PTO, which I would lose if I retired, and it felt like I was giving up so much. I was losing my position, steady income, and a platform to share the gospel. The uncertainties weighed heavily on me, yet I held onto my faith, trusting God to guide me through this transition.

God's guidance was evident from the start. He prompted me first to share my decision with the market president, who was also a Christian, and then with my reporting manager. Despite feeling nervous about how they would react, I followed God's instructions, even down to my announcement's specific date and details. I still had concerns about my PTO, as I stood to lose over 300 hours of unpaid time off. It was disheartening, especially since my manager had previously restricted me from taking any PTO, something that had never happened before.

However, God had a plan. When I reached out to HR, they explained an "80 Plan" for retirement benefits. This plan required having the sum of your age and years of service total of 80.

Miraculously, my age was 53, and my years of service were 27—exactly 80. It felt like divine intervention, affirming that this was God's timing for my retirement. Not only did I qualify for the retirement benefits, but I also received all my accumulated PTO and the bonuses for the quarters and the ending year I had worked.

Throughout this journey, I was in awe of how everything unfolded. I was anxious and uncertain, not knowing what the future would hold after leaving the security of my job and benefits. Yet, God continually reminded me of His promises, particularly through *Psalm 32:8 (NIV), which says, "I will instruct you and teach you in the way you should go; I will counsel you with my loving eye on you."*

This verse became a cornerstone of my faith, guiding me through the transition and reaffirming that God's promises are steadfast and true. God's presence was palpable, and I held onto His words daily, knowing He cannot lie and will always fulfill His promises. Even when the path ahead seems unclear, I trust that God's answers and solutions are always perfect and align with His greater plan for us.

God closed the door where I could no longer walk-through anymore. It became clear that He wanted me to retire, to position me for the next chapter of my life. I struggled with this realization, questioning why I could no longer continue my career. I was afraid, feeling unprepared for what lay ahead. But I knew deep down that God was closing this door for a reason. He was preparing me for something greater, a new beginning that required my complete trust in Him.

Despite my fears and doubts, I had to trust Him because He had closed the door. It was a clear sign that my time in this career was over and that He was guiding me toward the next step in my life. I leaned on *Jeremiah 29:11 (NIV), which says, "For I know the plans I have for you, declares the Lord, plans to prosper you and not to harm you, plans to give you hope and a future."* This verse became my anchor, reminding me that God had a plan for me, even if I couldn't see it at the moment.

I was scared but knew I had to trust His timing and plan. God was preparing me for the next chapter in my life, equipping me with valuable skills, knowledge, and experience that I would need. He had used my career to shape me, to teach me lessons that would be essential for my future.

I felt a profound sense of peace and contentment as I embraced retirement. I knew God had used my career to impact many lives and had more plans for me.

I was excited about the new adventures ahead and how God would continue to use me to share His love and hope with others.

Reflecting on my career and retirement, I am grateful for the incredible journey God has led me on. His timing is always perfect, and I trust He will continue to guide me in the future. I am thankful for the experiences and memories, the lives I touched, and how God used me to bring healing and hope to others.

# Chapter Three: Starting a Business in a Pandemic – God's Blessing

In the last few months, my life has undergone dramatic changes. I just turned 54 years old and never imagined simultaneously facing so many life-altering events. I went through a heart-wrenching divorce; I retired from a company that I had 27 years of dedication and commitment to, and I had relocated from Florida to Georgia, and yet, during all this turmoil, God opened another door for me that required complete trust in Him.

God's timing is impeccable, and His plans for us are always perfect, as it says in *Jeremiah 29:11-13 (NIV): "11 For I know the plans I have for you," declares the Lord, "plans to prosper you and not to harm you, plans to give you hope and a future. 12 Then you will call on me and come and pray to me, and I will listen to you. 13 You will seek me and find me when you seek me with all your heart."*

God had a plan for me that required me to trust and rely on Him completely. I didn't realize it then, but God had been preparing me all along. The experiences, knowledge, and education I gained over the years made me capable and ready to start my own business. It was January 2021 when I realized I couldn't stay retired long. I had always been a person who needed to stay busy, keep my mind occupied, and, most importantly, trust God with the new chapter in my life. God laid it on my heart that I could do it and that His plan for me was perfectly prepared.

I began to think about how I could make a difference and impact many lives while continuing to share the gospel. God inspired me to start my own consulting business. I have to admit I was nervous and afraid. The world was facing a pandemic; COVID-19 had shut everything down. We were confined indoors, and everything was done virtually. No one was meeting clients in person or conducting face-to-face training.

But I knew in my heart that I wanted to reach out to people and allow God to use me. In January 2021, I officially started as a CDR Financial Consultant. I was altogether nervous and unsure of how to approach clients. I knew my history and track record for partnership and relationship-building with previous organizations, but starting my own business was a different challenge. I trusted God and stepped out on faith, knowing that the same God who helped me grow over $71 million for the bank where I worked for over 27 years could also help me succeed in my business.

My first client was the Pinellas County Urban League. I contacted them because of our solid relationship and their mission to help small businesses succeed. I approached Watson Hayne, the president, and Charlotte Anderson, the COO, seeking a partnership and an opportunity to work with small business clients. I was nervous and unsure of God's plan because I didn't have a solid strategy. I wanted to help small businesses, especially during the pandemic.

Working in the financial sector, I noticed that many small business owners were not financially prepared to receive additional funding, and their businesses collapsed as a result. I remember praying to God, asking for a chance to help small businesses prepare for disasters. Despite living in Georgia and starting a business targeting Florida clients, I trusted God to open the necessary doors.

I pitched my ideas to the President and COO of the Pinellas County Urban League, relying on God to guide me through the process. *Isaiah 43:18-19 (NIV) says: "18 Forget the former things; do not dwell on the past. 19 See, I am doing a new thing! Now it springs up; do you not perceive it? I am making a way in the wilderness and streams in the wasteland."* This scripture resonated deeply within me as I realized I needed to forget the past and move forward. Despite my nerves and fears, God showed me that I was capable. I had run an $80 million business and had the experience to succeed. My faith helped me overcome the challenges of starting a new business.

I prayed constantly, read His word, and sought His guidance daily. Starting a business during a pandemic taught me to rely entirely on God. The world was shut down, and we had to rely on virtual networking and phone calls. But God provided a foundation for me, beginning with the Urban League, which helped me develop business plans and offered support. They were the stepping stones of my business journey.

God showed me that my business was not just about finance. As my business grew, I changed its name to CDR Consulting Services to reflect our broader scope of services. God revealed that I could do more than just finance—I could help small business owners identify gaps, provide coaching and mentoring, and prepare them for success. He also showed me the importance of leadership development and training.

With over 27 years of management experience, God used me to help others develop their careers. My business became a platform for ministry, allowing me to share the gospel with clients and colleagues. Walking in faith requires complete trust in God—not 50%, not 75%, not even 90%, but 100%. There were times I cried, prayed, and sought God's direction, and He always provided. Proverbs 3:5-6 (NIV) guided me: *"Trust in the Lord with all your heart and lean not on your own understanding; in all your ways submit to him, and he will make your paths straight."*

This verse became my lifeline. I understood that my business was a blessing from God, meant to minister to others. Meeting countless business owners and working with leaders in various fields, I shared God's gospel and witnessed the power of faith.

God taught me that the business He assigned me was not about money or making six or seven figures but about ministering to others. I met with countless business owners, trained and developed leaders, and shared God's message.

I wanted God to be pleased with how I represented Him and managed the business He entrusted me. I learned to trust Him completely, knowing He would provide, just as He had in the past.

Starting a business during a pandemic was challenging. Still, I knew that if God gave me this business during such a time, He would continue to provide. He brought clients, built relationships, and provided income. If you are considering starting a business, I encourage you to trust God. I trust Him today and will continue to trust Him, always aiming to be a good steward of the business He assigned to me.

I will always be grateful for the opportunity to share God's gospel through my work. The beauty of walking in faith with God is trusting Him completely. Despite the challenges, I know God is with me, guiding my steps and opening doors. His blessings during the pandemic showed me how much He cares and wants me to make a difference.

Today, I continue to share God's message, not afraid to let Him use me. The journey of faith is beautiful, and I will always thank God for this opportunity. My prayer is to always represent Him well and to trust Him with every step of my journey.

Trusting God, especially in times of uncertainty, is not just a decision but a continuous journey. Starting a business during a pandemic was an enormous leap of faith. Every step, from the initial idea to the actual launch, required a deep and unwavering trust in God's plan. This trust was not something I could muster up on my own; it was my faith built over time through prayer, reading the Bible, and seeing God's faithfulness in my life.

Each day presented new challenges and opportunities. I began my mornings with prayer, seeking God's guidance for the day ahead. I asked Him to open doors, connect me with the right people, and give me the wisdom to make sound decisions.

One particular morning, I felt overwhelmed by the number of tasks on my to-do list. As I prayed, I felt a sense of peace wash over me, reminding me of *Matthew 6:34 (NIV): "Therefore, do not worry about tomorrow, for tomorrow will worry about itself. Each day has enough trouble of its own."* This verse helped me focus on taking one step at a time and trusting that God would handle the rest. It wasn't always easy, but when I surrendered my worries to God, He provided exactly what I needed.

Financial uncertainty was one of my biggest challenges when starting my business. After 35 years of steady income as an employee, transitioning to a business owner meant relying on clients to pay for services rendered, often with delays of 30 to 45 days. This shift required a significant mindset change from depending on a regular paycheck to managing accounts receivable. It was a huge adjustment, especially during times when payments were delayed. I had to trust God completely to provide for both my business and personal expenses.

This faith was essential to navigate the financial uncertainties and maintain stability. Remembering the story of the widow's oil in *2 Kings 4:1-7 (NIV)* kept me grounded in managing my business and personal finances, where God provided abundantly from seemingly nothing.

Inspired by this story, I prayed for provision and wisdom in resource management. During times of low income and scarce new clients, I also leaned on another powerful scripture, which provided strength and reassurance: *Philippians 4:19 (NIV), "And my God will meet all your needs according to the riches of his glory in Christ Jesus."*

True to His word, God provided in miraculous ways. Unexpectedly, a contract I had nearly given up on came through, requiring assistance with coaching and training small business owners to help them achieve financial stability in their day-to-day operations.

This provision was a powerful reminder of God's faithfulness and His promise to meet our needs. Networking and building relationships are crucial in any business. However, with social distancing measures in place, traditional networking events were canceled. I had to rely on virtual meetings and phone calls. Initially, I was frustrated and doubted whether this approach would be effective. But God's word reminded me of *Ecclesiastes 3:1 (NIV)*: *"There is a time for everything and a season for every activity under the heavens."*

One memorable example was a virtual conference I attended on a whim. Though I had low expectations, I felt prompted to join. During one session, I connected with a fellow attendee who also provided consulting services for small business owners.

This connection became a significant template for reaching successful small business leaders with $10 million or higher sales revenue.

It reaffirmed that God's timing is perfect and that He can use any situation to our advantage. The pandemic forced many businesses to pivot and adapt. For me, this meant expanding my services and embracing new opportunities. Initially, I was hesitant. Change is often uncomfortable, and I worry about entering unfamiliar territory. But I remembered *Isaiah 41:10 (NIV): "So do not fear, for I am with you; do not be dismayed, for I am your God. I will strengthen you and help you; I will uphold you with my righteous right hand."*

Inspired by this promise, I started exploring new avenues for service. This led to expanding my consulting services to include online management and leadership training.

By embracing these opportunities, I was able to meet my clients' evolving needs and continue growing my business. One of the hardest lessons was learning to trust God with the outcome, regardless of my efforts. It's natural to want control and assurance, but faith requires us to let go and trust that God is in control. *Proverbs 16:9 (NIV)* became a cornerstone for me: *"In their hearts, humans plan their course, but the Lord establishes their steps."* This verse reminded me that while I can make plans and work hard, ultimately, it is God who directs my path. Sometimes, things didn't go as planned, and I faced setbacks. In those moments, I had to remind myself that God's ways are higher than my ways and His thoughts are higher than my thoughts *(Isaiah 55:8-9) (NIV)*.

As my business began to grow and make some progress, I suddenly had a setback: four major contracts fell through within two weeks. I was upset and questioned what I had done wrong. But through prayer and reflection, I realized God had a different plan.

This experience taught me to trust that God's plan is always for my good, even when it doesn't make sense at the moment.

Trusting God is a continual process of growth and learning. Each day brings new challenges and opportunities to rely on Him. One of the ways I've grown is by immersing myself in scripture and seeking wisdom through God's word. Passages like *Psalm 37:5-6 (NIV)* has been particularly encouraging: *"Commit your way to the Lord; trust in him and he will do this: He will make your righteous reward shine like the dawn, your vindication like the noonday sun."*

This commitment to trusting God has become the foundation of my business. I've learned that success is not just about financial gain but about being faithful to the mission God has given me. It's about positively impacting others and using my business as a platform to share God's love and truth. Starting a business during a pandemic has been one of my life's most challenging and rewarding experiences. It has stretched my faith, deepened my trust in God, and shown me the power of His provision and guidance.

Through every high and low, I've learned that trusting God is not just a one-time decision but a daily commitment. Suppose you are considering starting a business or facing challenges in your current venture. In that case, I encourage you to trust God wholeheartedly. Seek His guidance, rely on His promises, and be open to His leading. Remember that He is faithful, and His plans for you are good. Walking in faith, you will see His hand at work in ways you never imagined.

Starting my own business to share God's word fills my heart with deep gratitude and joy. This journey has been an incredible blessing, allowing me to spread the gospel through my work.

Trusting God has been the guiding force in navigating this challenging season, and it remains the foundation upon which I build my business. I pray that you, too, will find joy and peace in trusting God with every aspect of your life and work.

# Chapter Four: Battling Breast Cancer – God's Strength and Protection

Facing breast cancer for the second time was one of the most difficult, challenging, and devastating moments of my life. Confronting this monstrous disease again required me to trust God more deeply than ever before. It was a significant journey where I prayed, questioned, and sought answers from God. Why had the cancer returned? Why was I chosen again to fight this beast?

In those moments of anguish, God reminded me of *Joshua 1:9 (ESV): "Have I not commanded you? Be strong and courageous. Do not be frightened, and do not be dismayed, for the Lord your God is with you wherever you go."* This verse became my anchor. God quickly reminded me of His command to be strong and courageous, even in the face of such a daunting challenge.

Let me be clear: cancer is a beast. I want to share how God helped me battle breast cancer, how He gave me strength, and how He protected me through the entire ordeal. So many people are impacted by cancer, and the type that attacked me was breast cancer. Talking about it is still very painful; the hurt lingers, and sometimes I wonder why.

I am a two-time breast cancer survivor. It all began in 2015 when I was first diagnosed with stage 1 breast cancer. I was two months away from receiving my Bachelor of Applied Science degree, failing my classes, and not doing well in my courses. I remember my professor calling me, telling me to take care of myself and not to worry about school. But I knew if I could complete the last two months, I could get my degree and focus on fighting the cancer.

However, my body was tired, and the cancer was attacking me physically and mentally. I didn't have the capacity to handle school, work, and take care of my family. It was overwhelming, so I chose to withdraw from college to focus on my health and well-being. I had surgery in October 2015 and underwent 12 weeks of radiation treatments. After completing the treatments, I returned to school and eventually received my degree. For the next few years, I went for regular check-ups, and each time, the hematologist assured me that I was doing well.

But deep inside, I knew something was not right. I started experiencing severe side effects from the medication meant to prevent cancer recurrence. I had gained weight and was over 210 lbs., suffered from insomnia and depression, and lacked focus. The quality of my life deteriorated. In the second year of taking the medication, I decided to stop without consulting my family. I told myself that if cancer returned, it would be because God allowed it, and I would trust Him to guide me through it.

Fast forward to November 2022, during a self-examination of my breast, I noticed three red lumps on my left breast. I knew this was serious, so I reached out to my health plan agent, sharing my concern that the cancer might have returned. Unfortunately, the agent informed me that due to my condition being a recurrence, my health plan would not cover the costs. I was lost for words and scared, as I had been paying into this health plan for two years, not knowing they would not assist with medical expenses related to my condition.

The representative from the healthcare plan referred me to the United Cancer Support Foundation, a nonprofit based in Louisville, Kentucky. I contacted the organization and spoke with a kind woman named Mary. I explained my situation and that I needed a mammogram to determine if the cancer had returned. Mary informed me that their organization could assist with the mammogram, and I needed a hospital to conduct this examination.

She directed me to contact the Northside Hospital Center for Women's Diagnostics in Georgia. I immediately contacted the center and spoke with Anna, a Financial Counselor. I explained my situation but was informed by Anna that I needed a referral to proceed. Without a primary doctor in Georgia, I was at a loss.

Anna suggested that I get a referral from my previous hematologist in Florida. Knowing at this point, I was willing to pay out of pocket whatever the cost would be to find out if the cancer had reoccurred. I planned to pick up my mother from Florida a week before Thanksgiving. I knew time was against me getting a referral.

So, I contacted my doctor in Florida and explained the situation, and they kindly scheduled me for an appointment. Feeling stressed and overwhelmed, I flew to Florida that Sunday morning to prepare for my doctor's appointment on Monday.

My heart was heavy with worry as I met with the doctor on Monday, who carefully examined me and provided referrals for a mammogram, biopsy, and ultrasound.

The next morning, Tuesday, my mom and I drove back to Georgia for seven hours to spend Thanksgiving with the family, trying to focus on the time together despite the uncertainty and anxiety I felt.

My family was unaware this was happening to me again. After spending time with my family on Thanksgiving, I contacted Anna at Northside the next day but faced another hurdle; Anna shared with me that the nonprofit organization only covered the mammogram, not the ultrasound or the biopsy. At this moment in my life, I didn't know what else to do. I was seeking God, I was praying to God, and I felt as though every door kept closing.

But I knew that God did not close the doors. He wanted me to walk through the right doors. So, I started trusting Him even more because I knew God was going to work everything out for my good.

As it says in *Romans 8:28 (NIV)* [28] *And we know that in all things God works for the good of those who love him, who*[a] *have been called according to his purpose.*

Anna informed me that the hospital foundation offered financial assistance to patients like me who needed support due to a lack of health insurance coverage. She guided me through the process of applying for this assistance. To my immense relief, the Northside Hospital Foundation approved me for 100% financial assistance, enabling me to proceed with the diagnostic tests.

This support allowed me to undergo the necessary testing to determine if the cancer had returned. I underwent a mammogram, ultrasound, and a biopsy. In the midst of everything, I applied for a new healthcare insurance plan to ensure I was covered. However, the plan wouldn't begin until January 2023, leaving me feeling anxious and uncertain during the waiting period.

Throughout this process, I continued to trust God regardless of the outcome. I deeply believed God would hold my hand and guide me through this journey.

The tests confirmed my fears—I was diagnosed with stage two breast cancer. At that moment, my life seemed to come to a standstill. My son held me as I cried, and my sister offered comforting words. Dr. Robinson and Nurse Amy, who delivered the diagnosis, were incredibly kind and supportive, assuring me they would help me through this battle. They referred me to Dr. Erica Proctor, a breast cancer specialist at Northside Hospital.

Dr. Proctor was compassionate and thorough, explaining my options and the necessary steps. I chose to have both breasts removed to prevent any future recurrences.

She coordinated my care, connecting me with a plastic surgeon and a hematologist oncologist, Dr. Christopher Hagenstad.

I then faced another challenge; I discovered that plastic surgeons only accepted certain types of health insurance. I was in a state of limbo, needing to secure appropriate coverage quickly.

My previous insurance had denied my pre-existing condition, and my current insurance had rejected my claims from the hospital. In a moment of urgency, I reached out to the healthcare provider, explaining the critical need for surgery due to my breast cancer diagnosis. In a moment of grace, they provided the coverage I needed with another insurance, allowing the plastic surgeon and hospital to proceed with the necessary procedures, including a full mastectomy and reconstruction with a tummy tuck.

Throughout this challenging ordeal, I felt God's presence, guiding me through each closed door until we found the right path. I am deeply grateful for the strength and faith that sustained me.

I continually reminded myself of *Philippians 4:6 (NIV):* *"Do not be anxious about anything, but in every situation, by prayer and petition, with thanksgiving, present your requests to God."* This powerful scripture was my anchor, helping me to release worry and trust fully in God's plan as I navigated this difficult journey.

After my nine-hour breast surgery, I felt utterly defeated by the scars left on my body. I cried for months, unable to believe the ordeal my body had endured to fight breast cancer for a second time. The surgery left me with scars from my breast to my waistline, and every glance in the mirror reminded me of the battle. Facing these scars, I struggled to see any beauty.

Even as I lost my hair during chemotherapy, God was there, reminding me through scripture that I am fearfully and wonderfully made.

This experience has profoundly transformed me, forcing me to trust God truly. Breast cancer impacts you physically, mentally, spiritually, and emotionally. But God is rebuilding me with love, and though the scars remain, I now understand that He has made me fearfully and wonderfully, as stated in *Psalm 139:14 (NIV): "I praise you because I am fearfully and wonderfully made; your works are wonderful, I know that full well."*

Throughout this journey, God placed angels in my life—doctors, nurses, and my family. God tells us in *Exodus 14:14 (NIV), "The LORD will fight for you; you need only to be still."* God knew I could not fight this battle alone. *So,* God positioned my daughter to be able to move in with me and helped care for me for two months, supporting me through the most challenging times.

I had to learn to walk again, relying on my daughter to feed me, bathe me, and give me medicine. My son, daughter-in-law, sisters, and brother-in-law all took turns helping me with doctor visits and daily tasks. I trusted God through every step.

There were nights when I would wake up at 1 or 2 AM to walk through the house slowly and pray for strength. I sang hymns and recited *Isaiah 53:5: "But he was wounded for our transgressions, He was bruised for our iniquities: The chastisement of our peace was upon him, and with his stripes, we are healed."* This scripture kept my mind focused on Jesus and His healing power.

After the surgery and my healing process, it was time for Dr. Hagenstad, my hematologist and oncologist, to share a story about my journey with cancer and the necessity of chemotherapy. As he spoke, I felt a wave of hope and confidence wash over me for the treatment ahead. What was so amazing about Dr. Hagenstad was that no one had ever told me the story of my cancer journey in such a personal and heartfelt way. His words touched me deeply, breaking me down and making me realize the gravity of the fight I was enduring once again. But this time, I knew I wasn't alone. I felt a profound sense of peace, knowing that I didn't have to fight this battle by myself. God was with me, and all I needed to do was be still and trust in His presence and strength.

My cancer treatment included chemotherapy and radiation, which caused me to lose my hair—a significant concern for me. It felt like everything was being taken away from me—my marriage, my career, and my health. I feared that my appearance and identity were being stripped away. When I faced chemotherapy, I was terrified of the side effects and the physical toll it would take on my body. Additionally, I faced numerous challenges, including collapsing several times due to unknown causes. But God's grace was sufficient for me. Despite the fatigue and nausea, He provided moments of peace and relief. On days when I felt utterly weak, I would turn to 2 Corinthians 12:9 (NIV): "But he said to me, 'My *grace is sufficient for you, for my power is made perfect in weakness.'"* This verse reminded me that God's power was at its strongest in my weakest moments. In these times of vulnerability, I experienced His strength in the most profound way. Despite these setbacks, I trusted God to get me through. I knew that my battle was bigger than me, but my God was bigger than the disease.

After completing three months of chemotherapy, I contracted COVID, which delayed my radiation treatment. After 10 days of recovery from COVID-19, I began my radiation therapy. My faith was tested again when, a week before finishing my radiation treatment, I was diagnosed with shingles. Determined to complete my radiation on time, my doctors kindly allowed me to be the last patient to receive treatment, ensuring I could continue despite the challenges.

Again, God's grace was evident, helping me through this difficult time. No matter how many physical setbacks I faced, God was there for me, and I am very grateful for that.

Throughout this journey, I have been surrounded by professional, caring doctors, nurses, technicians, and lab personnel who made me feel supported and in the right place. I am deeply grateful for Northside Hospital and the incredible team God placed in my path. This experience has been a testament to God's provision and care, guiding me through every step of this challenging journey.

After seven years of being cancer-free, the cancer returned back in 2022, but I saw it as God's way of giving me a new beginning. Seven represents completion, and the eighth year represents a fresh start.

God gave me new health, strength, and renewed trust in Him.

In 2023, I began walking with God every day after my healing process. I read the entire Bible, learning more about who He is and falling in love with Him all over again. This journey taught me the importance of trusting God through every trial. It also gave me a different perspective of who He is in my life. Through my battle with breast cancer, I witnessed the power of God manifest in numerous ways. His presence was undeniable, and His strength became my sustenance. Each step of the way, I could see His hand guiding me, providing the right people and resources at just the right time.

God's power was also evident in His support system around me. My family, friends, and church community rallied around me, offering prayers, encouragement, and practical help. There were times when I felt isolated and overwhelmed by the weight of my diagnosis, but God used the people in my life to remind me that I was not alone. Their acts of kindness and words of encouragement were tangible expressions of God's love and care for me.

Prayer became my lifeline. In moments of fear and uncertainty, I would pour out my heart to God, seeking His comfort and guidance. *Psalm 46:1 (NIV) says, "God is our refuge and strength, an ever-present help in trouble."*

I clung to this promise, knowing God was my refuge in the storm. He was my source of strength when I felt like I had none left. Through prayer, I found peace that surpassed understanding, even in the midst of the chaos of cancer treatment.

God's provision was mind-blowing. From the nonprofit organization providing free mammograms to the compassionate doctors and nurses caring for me, God ensured I had everything I needed. When my insurance failed me, He opened doors I never could have imagined. He provided for my physical, emotional, and spiritual needs every step of the way.

As I reflect on my journey, I am reminded of the story of David and Goliath. David faced an insurmountable giant, but he trusted in God's power and defeated Goliath with a simple stone. Similarly, breast cancer was my giant, and though it seemed impossible to overcome, I trusted in God's power to see me through. Like David, I learned that it's not about the size of the giant but the size of our God.

My faith walks through cancer taught me the importance of surrendering to God's will. I learned to let go of my fears and doubts and to trust that God's plan for my life was good, even when I couldn't see it.

*Jeremiah 29:11 (NIV) says, "For I know the plans I have for you," declares the Lord, "plans to prosper you and not to harm you, plans to give you hope and a future."* This promise gave me hope and the assurance that God was in control.

To anyone facing physical or mental challenges, I encourage you to trust God. Walk with Him through your struggles. He is with you every step of the way, providing strength, healing, and protection. My journey through breast cancer was tough, but it brought me closer to God and revealed His incredible power and love. Remember this powerful scripture that got me through the most painful times of my life when I needed relief from physical and mental pain: *Matthew 11: 28-30 (NIV): "Come to me, all you who are weary and burdened, and I will give you rest.*

*Take my yoke upon you and learn from me, for I am gentle and humble in heart, and you will find rest for your souls. For my yoke is easy, and my burden is light."*

In the end, my battle with breast cancer was not just a physical fight; it was a spiritual journey. It was a walk of faith that deepened my relationship with God and strengthened my trust in His power and goodness. Through every trial and triumph, God was with me, guiding, strengthening, and showing me His incredible love.

# Chapter Five: Losing My Car in a Major Car Accident – God's Angels Protected Me

Life had thrown a relentless series of trials my way, each one seemingly more challenging than the last. Through every adversity, I walked with God, knowing that this journey of faith was essential for my growth and maturity as a believer. When I received the news in December 2022 about my breast cancer diagnosis, I knew I had to prepare myself for surgery in February 2023. I began to mentally and emotionally brace myself for the surgery ahead. However, I wasn't prepared for the next journey of faith that lay before me.

In January 2023, less than three weeks after being diagnosed with breast cancer, I faced yet another trial. A tractor-trailer semi-truck collided with my car, leaving me feeling as though everything was taken from me—

physically, mentally, spiritually, and emotionally. It was the lowest point of my life, and I felt utterly stripped of everything I had once known and relied upon.

In this moment of profound despair, I realized I had nothing left but to truly trust God and lean on Him in this faith walk. I clung tightly to His hand, holding on to His word, His promises, and, most importantly, His love for me. In this deep, dark valley, I learned the true essence of faith: trusting in God's love and plan, even when everything seems lost. This journey of trials and faith has been a testament to His unwavering support and a reminder that even in the darkest times, His love shines through.

In those darkest moments, I realized that God was positioning and preparing me for something greater. Despite feeling as though I had nothing left, I trusted in His plan. This unwavering faith allowed me to continue my journey, knowing that even in the midst of trials, God was with me, guiding me toward a brighter future.

Through this experience, I learned that true triumph comes not from avoiding hardships but from facing them with faith and trust in God's purpose for my life.

The day of the accident is seared into my memory. It was a rainy afternoon, and I had been spending the week with my granddaughter while her parents celebrated their birthdays. My daughter-in-law arranged for her sister to come over before 4 PM so I could head home before the traffic worsened.

As I set out on my journey home, the rain began to pour. I had my GPS on but chose to take a familiar route instead of following its directions. The highway was slick, and traffic was heavy. Suddenly, I saw the headlights of a semi-truck in my rearview mirror. The truck driver was merging into my lane, and no matter how much I sped up, he continued to edge closer. I was in the second right lane, and he was in the third lane.

Cars occupied the far-right lane, preventing me from moving over. In that tense moment, there were cars ahead of me, preventing me from speeding up to avoid the semi-truck that was dangerously close to hitting me. I did everything I could to get the driver's attention, signaling desperately to let him know he was merging into my lane.

Panicked, I blew my horn and yelled, "You're in my lane!" But the truck kept coming. Then, with a deafening boom, the semi hit my car on the driver's side. In that moment of impact, I heard God's voice telling me, "Do not hit the brakes." Obeying His command, I let my car spin across three lanes of traffic. It was 4 PM, the traffic was heavy, and it was raining. My car spun multiple times before becoming airborne and crashing into a ditch. I remember screaming, "Oh my God, oh my God," as my car rolled into a tree stump. The stump broke in half, with part of it wedging into the front driver's side of my car, stopping the vehicle.

In complete shock, I couldn't believe what had happened. I thought my life was ending. Smoke started to billow from the hood, and I prayed, "God, please don't let me die in this car. Don't let it catch fire. Help me get out."

I unlatched my seatbelt, crawled out of the car, and stood up, crying and screaming at the truck driver, who had continued down the highway but eventually stopped about half a mile away. I was utterly overwhelmed by what had just happened, collapsing several times in sheer emotional shock. I felt drained in every way—physically, mentally, spiritually, and emotionally. It seemed like I had nothing left in me to keep fighting this journey I was on. At that moment, it felt as though life itself was giving up on me. I couldn't understand why God had allowed this to happen to me, especially during a time when I was already dealing with so many other issues. But now, I had to find the strength to overcome this new challenge in my faith walk with God.

A UPS truck driver witnessed the accident and pulled over to help me. He kept asking if I was okay. I was in a state of shock, unable to process the fact that my car had spun multiple times on a busy highway without another vehicle hitting it. The UPS driver comforted me, keeping me calm until the paramedics arrived. The truck driver who hit me eventually came over, talking on his phone, trying to explain what had happened.

The paramedics took me to the hospital for examination. Unbelievably, I walked away with only a sore wrist from gripping the steering wheel so hard.

There were no broken bones or cuts. I walked out of that car accident alive because I listened to God's voice. Later, I learned from my attorney that if I had hit the brakes, the semi-truck would have rolled over my car, likely killing me.

The state trooper initially took the truck driver's side of the story, claiming I was merging into his lane. But I knew the truth. I prayed and trusted God to be my attorney and my witness.

Amazingly, the UPS driver had captured the accident on his dashcam, providing undeniable evidence of what had really happened. God had indeed sent His angels to protect me, slowing down the traffic just enough to prevent further collisions as my car spun out of control.

Reflecting on this experience, I realize the importance of having a relationship with Jesus Christ. This is why prayer and trust in God are crucial, no matter what challenges we face. This accident, combined with the many trials I had been through, including divorce, retirement, starting a business, relocating, and battling cancer, was the ultimate test of my faith. It broke me in ways I hadn't thought possible, strengthening my resolve to trust God's plan.

*Psalm 91:11-12 (NLT) says, "For he will order his angels to protect you wherever you go. They will hold you up with their hands, so you won't even hurt your foot on a stone."*
This scripture became my lifeline.

God's angels had indeed protected me that day, allowing me to walk away from what could have been a fatal accident.

In the end, the truck driver confessed, admitting his fault. God had seen everything, heard everything, and had been with me through it all. This journey has taught me to trust God completely. Despite the hardships, I learned that God's love is steadfast and His protection unfailing.

After completing my chemotherapy in June 2023 and following my surgery in February, God blessed me with a new beginning.

He upgraded my life in ways I couldn't have imagined. My old Toyota, which had been paid off, was replaced with a beautiful 2020 Mercedes-Benz—no car payments.

This was not just an upgrade in material terms but a symbolic representation of the new life and strength God had given me.

Throughout this journey, I realized the importance of facing adversity with faith. It is in these moments that God reveals His power and love. Every trial I faced was a step towards a greater understanding of who God is and how deeply He cares for His children. Like many other challenges, this accident was a testament to God's unwavering protection and love.

To anyone going through similar struggles, I encourage you to trust God fully. He sees your pain, knows your fears, and is always with you.

The trials we face are not meant to break us but to build us up to strengthen our faith and trust in Him. God's love is profound, and His plans for us are always for our good, even when we can't see it.

My story is a testimony of God's grace and protection. Despite the trials, He has been my rock, fortress, and deliverer. I am forever grateful for His love and the strength He has given me to endure and overcome. This journey has solidified my faith. I am committed to sharing His gospel and encouraging others to trust His perfect plan.

# Chapter Six: The Importance of Knowing God for Myself

Understanding and knowing God for yourself is paramount. This chapter emphasizes the critical importance of cultivating a personal relationship with God, especially through life's trials and tribulations. The role of God in your life, as well as mine, is the cornerstone of our faith walk and its results. As believers, we often try to impress the world. Still, we cannot have a fulfilling relationship with the world and expect to have a relationship with Jesus Christ simultaneously.

Our primary relationship must be with Jesus Christ, our Lord and Savior. Understanding God's nature—who He is, why He exists, and why we should have Him in our lives—is fundamental. Anytime I experience trials or tribulations, I reflect on the past three years of my life, from 2020 to 2023.

A lot has transpired during this period, and the benefits of knowing God have become increasingly clear to me. The trials I went through—my divorce, retirement, starting a business, being diagnosed with cancer for the second time, and having a car accident—were horrendous and life-changing. They were opportunities for me to grow, accept, and embrace the new beginning God had for me.

One of the foremost benefits I experienced was peace and comfort. Before I began enduring these trials, I lacked peace in my life. I was happy and content, but I didn't have true peace or comfort. God had to remove distractions from my environment to help me understand who He is and the importance of having Him as part of my life. These trials helped me overcome fears and anxieties.

We often don't realize we harbor fears and anxieties, but they are part of our human nature. A scripture I have read countless times but hadn't applied to my life became crucial: *Philippians 4:6-7 (ESV) - "Do not be anxious about anything, but in everything by prayer and supplication with thanksgiving let your requests be made known to God."* This scripture tells us not to fear, not to have anxieties, and not to worry. It is a command from God, a request that we are asked to follow.

During my faith walk, I had to apply this scripture many times. Did I worry sometimes? Yes, I did. Did I experience anxiety? Yes, I did. But the more I read, believed, and trusted God, the more I knew He had my back. This guidance came from reading God's Word daily, meditating on it, and seeking His direction. This didn't happen overnight; it took time, and God showed me how to fulfill the purpose He had for me.

Now, I completely understand the value and benefits of knowing God through any journey or faith walk. Knowing God personally is crucial because it establishes a deep, intimate relationship with Him. He wants us to believe in Him, love Him, and accept Jesus Christ as our Savior on a personal level.

Reading the Bible is essential for developing this relationship. The Bible is God's spoken word, filled with His teachings. It guides us from birth to death, instructing us how to live. One scripture that underscores this is *2 Timothy 3:16-17 (NIV)* - *"All Scripture is God-breathed and is useful for teaching, rebuking, correcting and training in righteousness, so that the servant of God may be thoroughly equipped for every good work."* This powerful scripture helps us understand why God provides His Word—to teach, rebuke, correct, and train us in righteousness.

I am not perfect, but God is here to help us correct our decisions and face trials. God has always been there for me throughout my life, but these last few years have deepened my understanding of the Holy Spirit. The Holy Spirit guides us when things are unclear, speaking to us and helping us navigate life's challenges. There have been countless times, especially in recent years, when I felt the Holy Spirit's guidance.

Before my breast cancer diagnosis, God was preparing me, telling me to read and trust His Word. In 2022, the Holy Spirit kept reminding me to stay focused on His word, preparing me mentally and spiritually for the journey ahead. I didn't fully understand then, but I continued to read, trust, meditate on, and pray about God's Word.

This preparation helped me develop a daily prayer and worship life. It was a different level of worship, where I had to honor God in every moment, even though my divorce, retirement, relocation, starting a business during a pandemic, being diagnosed with cancer for the second time, and losing my car in an accident. God showed me that He had to be first in my life.

I realized that many distractions had taken precedence over God. I was codependent on the world's perspective, not on God's perspective, His Word, or His love for me. Knowing God for myself became paramount.

No matter what you are going through, I challenge you to know God for yourself. Whether entering a trial, in the middle of one, or coming out of one, I recommend knowing God personally.

God's word is powerful. I didn't realize how much I needed to depend on the Holy Spirit and Jesus. God surrounded me with His angels, lifting me up when I couldn't walk or protect myself. This faith walk proved that God exists and that I can trust Him.

The journey was tough, difficult, and challenging, but God showed me that if He takes everything away, He will bless me with His plans. Trusting Him and giving me a new beginning, as mentioned in *Isaiah 43:18-19 (NIV)*, showed me that He was doing something great in my life, but I had to go through my faith walk to see it.

Prayer is a powerful tool in developing and maintaining a personal relationship with God. During these trials, I learned the importance of praying with God—moments to listen to Him, meditate on His word, and read the Bible to guide me. These moments of prayer became essential in navigating my journey. They provided the strength, guidance, and comfort I needed to face each day and overcome each challenge.

Dedicated time for prayer, meditation, and reading God's Word allows us to connect with God on a deeper level. In these moments, we can hear His voice, feel His presence, and understand His will for our lives. This practice helped me trust God more, lean on His understanding, and follow His path.

Trusting God during my faith walk had a profound impact on my life. It taught me to rely on Him, not my understanding of the world's perspective.

This trust brought peace, comfort, and a sense of security, knowing God was in control. It also provided clarity and direction, helping me make decisions aligned with His will.

In conclusion, knowing God for oneself is essential for a fulfilling and resilient faith walk. Through my journey, I have learned the importance of personal knowledge of God and the benefits that come with it. It has provided me with peace, comfort, and the ability to overcome fears and anxieties. It has deepened my understanding of God's nature and role in my life.

# Chapter Seven: Encouraging to Have a Personal Relationship with God

My faith in Jesus Christ as my Lord and Savior has been my anchor throughout my life, especially during the more challenging times. Through Him, I have found strength, hope, and perseverance. This chapter emphasizes the importance of having a personal relationship with God, which is only possible through Jesus Christ. It challenges you to embrace this transformative relationship.

The foundation of any personal relationship with God is faith in Jesus Christ. *Romans 10:9 (NIV) says, "If you declare with your mouth, 'Jesus is Lord,' and believe in your heart that God raised him from the dead, you will be saved."* This verse encapsulates the core of the Christian faith.

Through Jesus, we come to know God, experience His love, and receive His grace. My journey has been a testament to the power of faith in Jesus. There were times when I was overwhelmed by the trials before me—health challenges, emotional struggles, and moments of deep despair. Yet, my unwavering belief in Jesus Christ carried me through these difficult times. I was not alone; He was with me, guiding and sustaining me.

One of the most powerful ways to encourage others to seek a personal relationship with God is by sharing your own faith journey. I have encountered countless people, and sharing how God has worked in my life has been a source of inspiration for many. Whether it was how God orchestrated my path to receiving help for my breast cancer, preparing me for surgery, or aligning me with the right doctors, His handiwork was evident.

Sharing these experiences is crucial. It allows others to see the real impact of faith in one's life. It's not about boasting but testifying to God's goodness and grace.

It's about letting others know that trusting in Him can lead to miraculous outcomes and profound peace, even in the midst of trials.

While personal faith is vital, the role of the church community cannot be overstated. The church is not just a building; it is the collective body of believers who come together to worship, support, and uplift each other. My church community played an invaluable role in my faith walk. There were times when I couldn't physically attend church due to chemotherapy, surgery, and radiation. Still, the support from my church family was unwavering.

*Matthew 18:20 (ESV) states, "For where two or three are gathered in my name, there am I among them."* This scripture emphasizes the importance of fellowship.

Being part of a church community helps reinforce our faith, provides a support system, and reminds us that we are not alone in our walk with God.

God has a plan for each of us, and trusting in His plan is a crucial aspect of our faith walk. My journey has been life-changing, transforming me mentally, spiritually, physically, and emotionally. There were moments when I questioned why I had to endure so much, but looking back, I see God's hand in every step.

Believing in God's plan brings a sense of peace and contentment, especially during difficult times. It gives us a sense of purpose and fulfillment. My faith walk has taught me to overcome obstacles, trust God's plan, and not give in to fear or doubt. I had to familiarize myself with God's Word and let it guide me through my trials.

Prayer and meditation on God's Word are powerful tools that help maintain and deepen our faith. My war room—a space dedicated to prayer and communion with God—became my sanctuary. It was where I sought clarity, discernment, and understanding.

*Matthew 6:6 (NIV) says, "But when you pray, go into your room, close the door, and pray to your Father, who is unseen. Then your Father, who sees what is done in secret, will reward you."* This scripture underscores the value of private prayer and connection with God.

Understanding the power of prayer and meditation is essential for maintaining faith and receiving clarity from God. I have experienced firsthand how God provides clarity and guidance through His Word during trials. It's a practice that strengthens our relationship with Him and reinforces our trust in His plan.

Encouraging to have a personal relationship with God is not just about words; it's about living out our faith.

Our actions, how we treat others, and how we handle challenges speak volumes. Demonstrating God's love through our actions and sharing our personal relationship with Him can inspire others to seek the same.

God has a plan for all of us, and we must trust our faith walk. Support others going through their faith walks and remember that God's plan is the best for our lives.

My journey has been tremendously life-changing, and I am grateful for the support and prayers from my church community and loved ones.

In closing, I challenge you to understand the importance of personal relationships with God through Jesus Christ. Embrace the transformative power of faith, trust in God's plan, and stay committed to your faith walk. Share your journey with others, support those in need, and let your life be a testament to God's love and grace.

*Romans 10:9 (NIV) says, "If you declare with your mouth, 'Jesus is Lord,' and believe in your heart that God raised him from the dead, you will be saved."* This is the cornerstone of our faith. Declare your faith, believe in your heart, and experience the incredible walking journey with God.

Thank you for allowing me to share my story and testimony. I pray that you will understand the importance of a faith walk, recognize God's role in our lives, acknowledge Jesus Christ as our Lord and Savior, and appreciate the guidance of the Holy Spirit. Stay focused on God, His Word, and your faith walk with Him. Embrace the journey, for it is a journey that will lead you to unimaginable peace, joy, and fulfillment in the presence of our Lord and Savior, Jesus Christ.

# Conclusion:
# Choosing the Right Path:
# A Spiritual Reflection

As I reflect on my faith journey, I've learned that choosing the right path has been crucial in deepening my trust in God. The teachings of *Matthew 7:13-14* (NIV) have been a guiding light: *[13] "Enter through the narrow gate. For wide is the gate, and broad is the road that leads to destruction, and many enter through it. [14] But small is the gate and narrow the road that leads to life, and only a few find it."* This scripture challenges us to consider the paths we take in life. The wide gate represents the world's way, a path filled with ease but leading to destruction. In contrast, the narrow gate symbolizes the road less traveled, a path of righteousness that requires trust and reliance on God, especially during trials and tribulations.

Through my experiences, I've come to understand that the narrow gate is where God calls us to be. It's on this path that we learn to lean on Him, allowing our faith to grow and mature. So, as you walk your faith journey, I encourage you to reflect on your choices. Seek God's guidance to help you walk through the narrow gate, trusting in His plan for your life.

Be blessed with abundant blessings. Embrace your journey with faith, knowing that God's plan is to nurture and grow you in ways you cannot yet imagine. Enjoy the journey, and love the path God has set for you.

**Here are Several Vital Practices That Helped me Trust God in my Faith Walk:**

## Utilizing the Bible and Prayer

The Bible and prayer are indispensable tools in our faith walk. They serve as our spiritual compass, providing direction, wisdom, and comfort. Here's how to utilize these powerful resources:

### The Bible

The Bible is God's living word, a source of truth and guidance for every aspect of our lives. To truly trust God, we must immerse ourselves in His word. Here are some practical steps to incorporate the Bible into your daily life:

1. **Daily Reading:** Set aside time each day to read the Bible. Choose a reading plan or start with a specific book that resonates with your current situation.

2. **Meditation:** Reflect on the scriptures you read. Ask God to reveal His truths and how they

apply to your life.

3. **Memorization:** Commit key verses to memory. These scriptures will become your spiritual arsenal, ready to be recalled in times of need.

4. **Application:** Live out the principles and commands found in the Bible. Allow God's word to transform your thoughts, actions, and decisions.

## Prayer

Prayer is our direct line of communication with God. Through prayer, we express our deepest desires, fears, and gratitude. To develop a robust prayer life, consider the following:

1. **Consistent Schedule:** Establish a regular time for prayer each day. This helps create a habit of seeking God's presence.

2. **Honesty:** Be open and honest with God about your feelings and struggles. He desires a

genuine relationship with you.

3. **Listening:** Take time to listen to God's voice. Prayer is a two-way conversation, and God often speaks through the stillness of our hearts.

4. **Intercession:** Pray for others, raising their needs and concerns. This will bless them and strengthen your own faith.

## Drawing Closer to God

The trials I faced drew me closer to God, teaching me the importance of dependence on Him. Each challenge was a reminder of my need for His strength and guidance. Through these experiences, I learned valuable lessons about faith and trust:

1. **God's Faithfulness:** Despite the difficulties, God remained faithful. He provided comfort, strength, and direction, proving He is trustworthy.

2. **Dependence on God:** Trials taught me to rely on God rather than my own understanding or abilities. This dependence deepened my relationship with Him.

3. **Growth and Maturity:** Each challenge contributed to my spiritual growth, helping me mature in my faith and develop a deeper trust in God.

# Contact Info

## Resource Page

"BibleGateway." *BibleGateway.com: A Searchable Online Bible in over 150 Versions and 50 Languages.* www.biblegateway.com/

## Connect with Me

Email: cdrboss2019@gmail.com

Phone: 727-637-6846